MICHELANGELO

First edition for the United States, Canada,
and the Philippines published 1994
by Barron's Educational Series, Inc.

Design David West Children's Book Design
Compiled and researched by Gillian Bainbridge BA Hons, ATC

© Copyright by Aladdin Books Ltd 1993

Designed and produced by
Aladdin Books Ltd
28 Percy Street
London W1P 9FF

All inquiries should be addressed to:
Barron's Educational Series, Inc.
250 Wireless Boulevard
Hauppauge, NY 11788

International Standard Book No. 0-8120-1827-3

Library of Congress Catalog Card No.93-2384

Library of Congress Cataloging-in Publication Data
Hart, Tony, 1925-
Michelangelo / by Tony Hart. –1st U.S. ed.
p. cm. – (Famous children.)
Summary: Focuses on the childhood of the noted artist Michelangelo.
ISBN 0-8120-1827-3
1. Michelangelo Buonarroti, 1475-1564–Childhood and youth–Juvenile literature. 2.
Artists–Italy–Biography–Juvenile literature. [1. Michelangelo Buonarroti,
1475-1564–Childhood and youth. 2. Artists.] I. Title. II. Series.
N6923.B9H44 1993
709'.2--dc20   93-2384
[B]   CIP   AC
Special thanks to: The Bridgeman Art Library; Staatliche Graphische Sammlung,
Munich; Scala, Florence. The publishers have made every effort to contact
all the relevant copyright holders and apologize for any omissions that
may have inadvertently been made.
Printed in Belgium·
34 98765432

Famous Children

MICHELANGELO

TONY HART
ILLUSTRATED BY SUSAN HELLARD

BARRON'S

In the town of Caprese in Italy, during the spring of 1475, Francesca Buonarroti gave birth to her second son.

"We'll call him Michelangelo," announced the boy's father proudly.

Soon afterwards, Lodovico Buonarroti's job as Mayor of Caprese came to an end and the family packed  up their belongings to return home. The baby, Michelangelo, traveled with his parents to the family home in Florence and from there to Settignano, a village outside the town, where he lived with his nurse.

The countryside all around Settignano was very rich in stone. Quarries were everywhere, mined by stonecutters and sculptors.

Since his nurse's father and husband were both stonemasons, little Michelangelo grew up surrounded by chisels and hammers.

"You will soon know all about stone carving, Michelangelo," joked his nurse.

As Michelangelo played among the stones and quarries of Settignano, his family grew. Three more sons were born to Francesca and Lodovico. But sadly, when Michelangelo was six years old, his mother died.

Four years later, Lodovico married again. Michelangelo returned to Florence to join the family. He shared a gloomy house with his father, his stepmother, four brothers, and an uncle.

Michelangelo's father didn't earn much money. Some of his sons had to help out and were sent to work for silk and wool merchants. Michelangelo, though, went to school.

When his father realized that Michelangelo spent his time at school drawing instead of studying, he became very angry.

"You are wasting time on art. You will never make any money for yourself or for the family."

Michelangelo had been given the chance to become a scholar, but all he wanted to do was draw!

He became friendly with a local boy called Francesco Granacci. Francesco had been sent as a boy to learn the art of painting from Domenico Ghirlandaio, a famous local artist.

"You have great talent," said Francesco when he saw Michelangelo's work. "I will help you with your studies."

Michelangelo was delighted.

Every day Francesco would
bring one of Domenico's drawings
for Michelangelo to study and copy.

Michelangelo became better
and better until his father realized
that there was no hope of forcing his son
to give up drawing.

"I give in. You shall put these
talents to good use and learn
art properly," sighed his
father.

Michelangelo
couldn't wait to tell
Francesco that he would
soon be joining him.

Michelangelo became apprenticed to Domenico when he was thirteen years old. He learned the difficult technique of "fresco," painting on wet plaster.

"This is excellent, Michelangelo. You are improving at an astonishing rate," gasped Domenico.

He soon allowed the eager young apprentice to work with him on public frescoes. This was considered a great honor for Michelangelo.

Age 13

Michelangelo was still only thirteen when he painted a kneeling figure in Domenico's fresco of *The Baptism of Christ.*

One day Michelangelo watched an apprentice copy a drawing of Domenico's.

Michelangelo took the drawing and, using a thicker pen, went over the lines and improved it.

"You are better than our master!" exclaimed the apprentice.

Domenico himself was often surprised by Michelangelo. One day when they were working together in a chapel, Michelangelo started to sketch.

He drew what he saw around him – the scaffolding, trestle tables, stools, and materials, as well as all the men working there. When Domenico saw what Michelangelo had done, he was astonished.

"This boy knows more than I do!" he shouted with excitement.

Michelangelo was always searching for new ideas. He made a perfect copy in pen and ink of an engraving by a famous German artist. It showed St. Anthony being tormented by devils.

Michelangelo wanted to add color to the drawing.

"I need some help with the colors of the demons. I know – I'll look at some fish to see the fantastic colors of the scales."

Michelangelo also made excellent copies of the works of other famous artists such as Giotto and Masaccio.

"I shall tinge them with smoke; then they will look old and exactly like the original drawings," thought Michelangelo. And they did.

News of the boy's talents began to spread.

Age 13

Age 13

Lorenzo the Magnificent lived in the Medici Palace in Florence. He was the ruler of Florence and a great art lover and collector. He sent a message to Domenico.

"Send me your best pupils to study with the famous sculptor, Bertoldo, in my Sculpture Garden."

Domenico felt very honored by Lorenzo's request and immediately sent, among others, both Michelangelo and Francesco. Michelangelo was fascinated by the wonderful sculptures he saw there. He longed for the chance to make one himself.

With a few days, Michelangelo began a marble copy of an antique faun's head that he found in the garden. The face was very old, with wrinkles. It had a damaged nose and a laughing mouth.

This was the first time Michelangelo had worked with marble, but the copy was excellent. Lorenzo was walking through the garden, watching the boys at work. He saw the faun and was very impressed.

Then Lorenzo noticed that Michelangelo had given the faun a tongue and all its teeth. He laughed and said,

"But you should have known that old men never have all their teeth. Some of them are always missing."

Michelangelo took this criticism very seriously and, anxious to please Lorenzo, he broke one of the faun's teeth and dug a hole in the gum so that it looked as if the tooth had fallen out.

"Please, Sir, is this better?" he asked hopefully.

Lorenzo laughed even more.

"It is perfect!" he exclaimed.

Lorenzo decided to help young Michelangelo. He sent for the boy's father and asked whether Michelangelo could stay at the palace.

"I shall look after him as if he is one of my own sons," he promised.

His father willingly agreed and Michelangelo, now fifteen years old, was given his own room at the palace and ate all his meals with Lorenzo's family. And most important of all – he was given the keys to the Sculpture Garden.

Michelangelo worked hard. Other students began to envy his talent. A friend of Michelangelo's became so jealous that he punched him in the nose, breaking it.

During his stay at the Medici Palace, Michelangelo carved many pieces of marble.

"His work is so beautiful that it is almost impossible to

Age 16

believe it's the work of a young man and not a great master," said Lorenzo.

In 1492, when Michelangelo was seventeen years old, Lorenzo died. Michelangelo was filled with sorrow at the death of his generous friend.

Age 16

Michelangelo returned to live with his father, now in Rome. The following year he bought a large block of marble and carved a statue of "Hercules," eight and a half feet high, in memory of Lorenzo de Medici the Magnificent.

Lorenzo's son, Piero de Medici, was a great friend to Michelangelo, too, and would ask his advice about buying antiques.

One winter it snowed heavily in Florence and he asked Michelangelo,

"Can you make a statue out of snow?"

Michelangelo made a beautiful snow sculpture in Piero's courtyard. Everyone was amazed and Piero praised Michelangelo so highly that even Lodovico had to admit that his son was someone very special indeed.

Michelangelo lived for nearly 90 years and created some of the most beautiful works of art the world has ever seen.